MOUNTAIN
LIFE

Consultants : Ronald M. Nowak, George E. Watson
Illustrators: Barbara Gibson, Tim Phelps

Published by
The National Geographic Society
John M. Fahey, Jr., President and Chief Executive Officer
Gilbert M. Grosvenor, Chairman of the Board
Nina D. Hoffman, Senior Vice President
William R. Gray, Vice President and Director, Book Division

Staff for this Book
Barbara Lalicki, Director of Children's Publishing
Barbara Brownell, Senior Editor and Project Manager
Marianne R. Koszorus, Senior Art Director and Project Manager
Toni Eugene, Editor
Alexandra Littlehales, Art Director
Catherine Herbert Howell, Writer-Researcher
Susan V. Kelly, Illustrations Editor
Jennifer Emmett, Assistant Editor
Mark A. Caraluzzi, Director of Direct Response Marketing
Vincent P. Ryan, Manufacturing Manager
Lewis R. Bassford, Production Project Manager

Visit our Web site: www.nationalgeographic.com

Library of Congress Catalog Card Number: 97-76354
ISBN: 0-7922-3455-3

Color separations by Quad Graphics, Martinsburg, West Virginia
Printed in Mexico by R. R. Donnelley & Sons Company

MY FIRST POCKET GUIDE

MOUNTAIN LIFE

CATHERINE HERBERT HOWELL

All photographs supplied by Animals Animals/Earth Scenes

NATIONAL
GEOGRAPHIC
SOCIETY

INTRODUCTION

What makes a mountain a mountain? A mountain is a landform that rises at least a thousand feet above the surrounding land. It usually has a wide base and a peak or ridge at the top. North America has mountains ranging to 20,320 feet, the height of Alaska's Mount McKinley.

If you've ever hiked up a mountain, you may have noticed that the climate changes—it gets colder as you go higher. Near the top of tall mountains it may be very cold and windy, even in summer. This often makes living in mountains a challenge for animals. Animals adapt to mountain life in several ways. Mountain goats grow thick shaggy coats in winter to keep them warm on the rugged cliffs they call home. Some animals, such as the snowshoe hare, change color with the seasons, growing white winter coats that help them hide from predators in snow.

Other animals, such as elk, spend the summer on high meadows and come

down to sheltered forests in the winter.
Some birds nest in the mountains but
migrate, or move to a different area, in
the winter.

Many mountain animals are shy and hide
much of the time. You may see them—if
you are quiet and look carefully!

HOW TO USE THIS BOOK

This book is organized by type of animal.
First you will meet amphibians and reptiles,
then birds, and finally, mammals. Each
spread helps you to identify one
kind of animal and tells
you about its size, color,
and behavior. A paw or
hoof print indicates the
track made by a mammal.
A shaded map of North
America shows where to
find the animal, and the
"Field Notes" entry gives
an additional fact about
it. If you see a word you
don't know, look it up
in the Glossary on
page 76.

ENSATINA SALAMANDER

 Look for an ensatina (en-suh-TEE-nuh) salamander under a log. There it eats worms, spiders, and insects. Ensatinas, unlike many other amphibians, live entirely on land.

WHERE TO FIND:
Ensatina salamanders are found mostly in cool forests and shady canyons in western coastal mountains.

WHAT TO LOOK FOR:

✳ SIZE
Ensatinas grow from three to almost six inches long, including the tail.

✳ COLOR
They are brown or black with cream, yellow, or orange spots or blotches.

✳ BEHAVIOR
When threatened, an ensatina stands up, arches its back, and swings its tail.

✳ MORE
It has no lungs, but can breathe through its skin and the lining of its mouth.

The ensatina's body narrows at the base of the tail, where it breaks off if grabbed. The tail grows back right away.

○○○○○○○○○○○○○○○○

FIELD NOTES

When an ensatina's tail comes off, it keeps wiggling and confuses the attacker.

RED SALAMANDER

The red salamander is a shy, secretive amphibian that lives alone. It usually doesn't travel far from the stream where it hatched from its egg. At night it searches for earthworms, its favorite food.

FIELD NOTES

As it grows older, this salamander's bright color fades, and the amphibian becomes duller and brownish.

This black-chinned red salamander has a very dark chin. Its bright color suggests that it is young.

WHERE TO FIND:
Red salamanders live in leaf litter or under rocks and logs near streams in the eastern United States.

WHAT TO LOOK FOR:

✳ SIZE
Red salamanders reach four to seven inches in length.

✳ COLOR
They are red or reddish orange with dark spots.

✳ BEHAVIOR
Red salamanders hide under leaves to survive mountain winters.

✳ MORE
Like ensatina salamanders, they are lungless and breathe through their skin.

WESTERN TOAD

A western toad sounds like a baby chick peeping. This amphibian lacks a vocal sac, a pouch under the chin that fills with air and helps most other kinds of male toads croak loudly.

FIELD NOTES

A toad doesn't have to chase its dinner. It uses its long tongue to reach out and zap an insect.

Behind each eye the western toad has an oval gland that produces a poison. It makes the toad taste bad to predators.

WHERE TO FIND:
Western toads live in many habitats, including mountain meadows, in the western U.S. and Canada.

WHAT TO LOOK FOR:

✳ SIZE
The western toad grows to five inches.

✳ COLOR
It has many reddish warts outlined in black and a light stripe running down its back.

✳ BEHAVIOR
Like other amphibians, toads live on land but can breathe in water.

✳ MORE
It is not true that you can get warts from touching a toad.

SHORT-HORNED LIZARD

Though small, the short-horned lizard looks pretty ferocious. Short spines poke from its head and sides. When threatened, this reptile may hiss, bite, and even spurt blood from the corners of its eyes.

FIELD NOTES

To get away, a short-horned lizard shuffles from side to side and buries itself in sand or dirt.

Female short-horned lizards give birth to live babies, as many as 30 at a time.

WHERE TO FIND:
Short-horned lizards live in high mountain forests and in many other habitats in western North America.

WHAT TO LOOK FOR:

✳ SIZE
Short-horned lizards grow from a little over two to more than five inches long.

✳ COLOR
They are brownish with short spines and large dark spots on the neck.

✳ BEHAVIOR
Short-horned lizards are active mostly during the day, when they search for ants, their preferred food.

✳ MORE
They even eat small snakes.

COLLARED LIZARD

When an intruder bothers it, the collared lizard may open its mouth wide to show the dark lining inside. If that doesn't scare the enemy away, this fierce little reptile may bite—hard.

WHERE TO FIND:
Collared lizards are found on rocky ledges in hilly regions of North America.

WHAT TO LOOK FOR:

✳ SIZE
Collared lizards range from 8 to 16 inches in length, including the tail.

✳ COLOR
They are tan, yellowish, greenish, or bluish with dark or light spots.

✳ BEHAVIOR
Collared lizards often sit on rocks and rock ledges to soak up the warmth of the sun.

✳ MORE
Males have very large heads.

A male, such as this one, has two black rings around its neck. Females don't always have these rings.

15

RED-BELLIED SNAKE

 Though they are called red-bellied, these snakes may also have orange, yellow, or even black undersides. A shy creature of mountain woodlands, this reptile curls its upper lip when frightened.

WHERE TO FIND:
Look for red-bellied snakes in high woodlands or bogs, mainly in the eastern United States.

WHAT TO LOOK FOR:

✷ SIZE
Red-bellied snakes range in length from 8 to 16 inches.

✷ COLOR
They are brown, gray, or black with red, orange, black, or yellow bellies.

✷ BEHAVIOR
They often hide under piles of lumber or trash around houses.

✷ MORE
Females give birth to as many as 21 babies at a time.

When it loops itself into a coil, a red-bellied snake displays its two-toned body.

COPPERHEAD

 Lying coiled on a pile of dead leaves, the copperhead is almost invisible because of its coloring. It waits patiently for a mouse or other small animal to come close—and become its dinner.

WHERE TO FIND:
Copperheads live among rocks in wooded mountains and in other habitats in the southeastern United States.

WHAT TO LOOK FOR:

✳ SIZE
Copperheads range from 22 to 53 inches in length.

✳ COLOR
Their bodies are tan with dark hourglass patterns.

✳ BEHAVIOR
The snake uses its forked tongue to help it gather smells from the air.

✳ MORE
The copperhead has long, hollow fangs that inject poison.

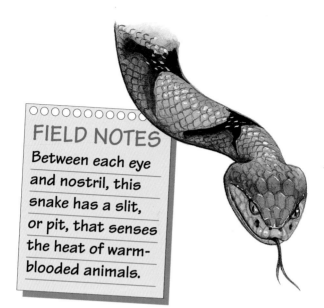

Copperheads, like other poisonous snakes known as pit vipers, have triangular heads.

TIMBER RATTLESNAKE

 When a timber rattlesnake feels threatened, it shakes the end of its tail. The message is: "I'm trouble." Like the copperhead, the rattler is a pit viper.

WHERE TO FIND:

Timber rattlers live on rocky, wooded mountains and hillsides as well as in lower swampy areas.

WHAT TO LOOK FOR:

✳ **SIZE**
Timber rattlers grow from about three to six feet long.

✳ **COLOR**
Their bodies vary from black to brown, gray, tan, or yellow with dark blotches.

✳ **BEHAVIOR**
In winter timber rattlers often gather together in a rocky den.

✳ **MORE**
When it molts—or sheds its skin—each year, a rattler grows a new tail segment.

Rattlesnakes usually don't strike unless disturbed. Stay alert when hiking in rocky places.

MOUNTAIN CHICKADEE

In mountain forests this chickadee searches for the insects it constantly eats. It finds most of them in the outer branches of conifers, or cone-bearing trees.

WHERE TO FIND:
Mountain chickadees live in woodlands with conifers in western parts of Canada and the United States.

WHAT TO LOOK FOR:

✱ SIZE
The mountain chickadee is a little more than five inches long.

✱ COLOR
It has a gray back and paler breast and body. Its chin, throat, and cap are black. Its cheeks and eyebrows are white.

✱ BEHAVIOR
In winter it may feed in large flocks with other kinds of small birds.

✱ MORE
Its call is a hoarse *chick-adee-adee-adee*.

You can tell a mountain chickadee from other chickadees by the white streak it has above each eye.

23

AMERICAN PIPIT

 While many birds hop to travel on the ground, the American pipit usually walks. Bobbing its tail as it goes, the pipit snatches insects and small seeds from the grass. It also feeds on insects frozen in snowbanks.

WHERE TO FIND:
American pipits summer on mountain meadows and tundra and migrate to fields and beaches in winter.

WHAT TO LOOK FOR:

✷ SIZE
The American pipit is about 6 and a half inches long.

✷ COLOR
It is brownish gray above and tan below with dark streaks.

✷ BEHAVIOR
It travels in enormous flocks while migrating.

✷ MORE
This bird is also called a water pipit because it is often found near water.

American pipits build nests of grasses and twigs on mountaintops and Arctic tundra.

WHITE-CROWNED SPARROW

 A small, slender bird, the white-crowned sparrow is known for the bold black and white stripes on its head. It stands straighter and taller than most other sparrows.

WHERE TO FIND:
It inhabits tundra and brush in mountains in summer, and lives in woodlands and parks in winter.

WHAT TO LOOK FOR:

✳ SIZE
White-crowned sparrows are about seven inches long.

✳ COLOR
They are brown above with dark streaks, gray undersides, and pointed pink or yellow bills.

✳ BEHAVIOR
They have different songs depending on which region they inhabit.

✳ MORE
In some areas they sing all night.

A pool mirrors the distinct head markings and bills of two white-crowned sparrows.

WESTERN TANAGER

 One of the most colorful birds in the Rocky Mountains, the western tanager is bold, too. As western tanagers fly south to their winter homes, they often feed in farmers' orchards.

WHERE TO FIND:
Western tanagers are found mainly in coniferous forests in summer. They migrate south for the winter.

WHAT TO LOOK FOR:

✳ SIZE
This tanager is about seven inches long.

✳ COLOR
The male has a bright red head and yellow body with a black back, wings, and tail. The female is yellow with a greenish back and wings.

✳ BEHAVIOR
The female builds the nest.

✳ MORE
A nest is made of twigs, pine needles, and moss and is lined with hair.

The bird feeds on insects and seeks out berries and other fruits when they ripen.

MOUNTAIN BLUEBIRD

Mountain bluebirds live in pairs. In the summer, a male and female build their nest in a tree, often in an old woodpecker hole. They work all day to catch insects for their five or six chicks.

Mountain bluebirds catch and eat a lot of insects, but they also perch to feed on seeds and berries.

WHERE TO FIND:
Mountain bluebirds inhabit high meadows and plains as well as grasslands in western North America.

WHAT TO LOOK FOR:

❋ **SIZE**
Mountain bluebirds are about seven inches long.

❋ **COLOR**
Males have sky blue backs and paler underparts. Females are mostly gray with bluish wings and tails.

❋ **BEHAVIOR**
Like other bluebirds, mountain bluebirds will build nests in nest boxes.

❋ **MORE**
They catch insects while in flight.

GRAY JAY

If you have something, a gray jay may want it. This bold bird visits campsites throughout its range, helping itself to food—baked beans are a favorite—and any other objects it finds interesting.

Though they like the food we eat, gray jays also eat many kinds of insects, mice, seeds, and berries.

WHERE TO FIND:

Gray jays live in coniferous forests in the mountains and northern areas of the United States and Canada.

WHAT TO LOOK FOR:

✳ SIZE

Gray jays are about 12 inches long.

✳ COLOR

They are mostly gray with black on their heads or necks and white cheeks.

✳ BEHAVIOR

They are noisy birds. They call, whistle, and scream.

✳ MORE

They store extra food by gluing it into balls with saliva and hiding it.

CLARK'S NUTCRACKER

Named for famous explorer William Clark, this nutcracker lives high up in the mountains. Its harsh call of *kra-a-a* rings out through the forests.

WHERE TO FIND:
Clark's nutcrackers are found in mountain pine forests in western Canada and the United States.

WHAT TO LOOK FOR:

✱ SIZE
The Clark's nutcracker is about a foot long.

✱ COLOR
It has a gray body, black wings, and a black tail with white sides.

✱ BEHAVIOR
The birds nest before winter ends and protect eggs and young from the cold.

✱ MORE
They prefer pine seeds, but also eat insects, eggs, and young birds.

The bill of the Clark's nutcracker is a combination pick, hammer, and ax it uses to crack open pinecones.

The favorite food of the Clark's nutcracker is the sweet nut of the piñon pine.

WHITE-TAILED PTARMIGAN

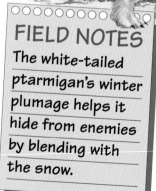

While other birds leave the high mountains in winter, the plump white-tailed ptarmigan (TAR-mih-gun) stays put. Its plumage turns white, and more feathers grow on its legs and feet to help keep it warm.

FIELD NOTES

The white-tailed ptarmigan's winter plumage helps it hide from enemies by blending with the snow.

In summer the white-tailed ptarmigan is a speckled brownish black that matches its rocky habitat.

WHAT TO LOOK FOR:

✳ SIZE
White-tailed ptarmigans are slightly more than 12 inches long.

✳ COLOR
Their mottled, brownish black summer plumage turns white in winter.

✳ BEHAVIOR
Groups may huddle together in snowstorms for protection.

✳ MORE
Above each eye is a fleshy red comb.

COMMON RAVEN

In Native American stories the raven is a clever character. In real life this large black bird is smart, too. For example, one member of a hungry pair tweaked a dog's tail while the other stole its food.

You can tell a raven from a crow by the raven's larger head, long thick bill, and wedge-shaped tail.

WHERE TO FIND:
Ravens live in mountains, coniferous forests, deserts, and along rocky coasts in much of North America.

WHAT TO LOOK FOR:

✳ SIZE
The raven is about two feet long.

✳ COLOR
It is all black—from its large shaggy head to the tip of its tail.

✳ BEHAVIOR
The raven often rides the wind, circling for hours like an eagle.

✳ MORE
Ravens build their nests in trees or on the sheltered ledges of cliffs.

FIELD NOTES

The acrobatic raven sometimes drops from the sky in a series of somersaults called barrel rolls.

BALD EAGLE

 Not long ago, majestic bald eagles nearly disappeared from many parts of North America. Now they are returning because laws have banned pesticides that got into their food and weakened their eggshells.

WHERE TO FIND:
Bald eagles are found near rivers and lakes, in mountain areas, and along coasts.

WHAT TO LOOK FOR:

✳ SIZE
Bald eagles are about three feet long.

✳ COLOR
Adults have dark bodies, white heads and tails, and yellow bills.

✳ BEHAVIOR
These eagles build huge nests, adding material each year until the nest may weigh a ton.

✳ MORE
Bald eagles eat fish, waterbirds, and even carrion.

Using sharp eyesight to spot a fish from great heights, the bald eagle swoops down on its prey.

It takes a bald eagle several years to develop the white head and yellow bill of an adult. Young eagles are all brown.

41

GOLDEN EAGLE

 Golden eagles are swift and mighty hunters. They often soar with wings slightly uplifted. They can snatch birds out of the air and lift bounding rabbits off the ground in an instant.

FIELD NOTES

Golden eagles frequently build nests on very steep cliffs to keep their eggs and young safe.

A golden eagle perches above its domain. It may defend a nesting territory of up to 75 square miles.

WHERE TO FIND:
Golden eagles are found in mountains and hilly regions throughout much of North America.

WHAT TO LOOK FOR:

❋ SIZE
Golden eagles grow 30 to 40 inches long. Females are larger than males.

❋ COLOR
Adults are dark brown and have gold-colored feathers on the backs of their heads and necks.

❋ BEHAVIOR
They hunt over open ground for small mammals, snakes, and other birds.

❋ MORE
Golden eagles take five years to mature.

WILD TURKEY

 Male wild turkeys, or toms, "strut their stuff" to attract mates. Fluffing their feathers and fanning their impressive tails, they often compete with each other for the attention of females.

WHERE TO FIND:
Wild turkeys live in brush and woodlands in mountain areas and other parts of North America.

WHAT TO LOOK FOR:

✳ SIZE
Male turkeys grow to four feet long. Females are about a foot shorter.

✳ COLOR
Males have brown feathers with a rich red and green gloss. Females are duller.

✳ BEHAVIOR
Wild turkeys forage on the ground for insects, acorns, seeds, and berries.

✳ MORE
They can fly up to 55 miles an hour for short distances.

FIELD NOTES

Although large, the turkey is a fast runner and can even outpace a fox. The birds can also swim.

Only the male turkey has a big wattle—red skin that dangles from its head and neck.

PIKA

 With short, rounded ears, stubby legs, and no tail, the pika looks more like a mouse than a rabbit, its closest relative. The soles of its feet are furry to keep it warm in winter and to keep it from slipping.

WHERE TO FIND:
Pikas inhabit rocky slopes in the mountains of western Canada and the United States.

WHAT TO LOOK FOR:

✳ **SIZE**
The pika ranges from six to almost nine inches in length.

✳ **COLOR**
Its fur is brown and very thick.

✳ **BEHAVIOR**
Pikas call out with a loud nasal bark when danger threatens.

✳ **MORE**
These mammals remain active throughout the long, cold winter.

FIELD NOTES

In summer pikas gather plants and grasses, let them dry like hay, and store them as food for winter.

Pikas stuff their summer hay under rock ledges and stand guard in front to keep other animals away.

47

RED SQUIRREL

If another animal enters a red squirrel's area, it will hear about it. Red squirrels actively defend their territories. They loudly scold and threaten trespassers and chase intruders away.

This squirrel's reddish coat becomes duller in winter.

WHAT TO LOOK FOR:

✳ SIZE
The red squirrel is up to 14 inches long, including its 5- to 6-inch tail.

✳ COLOR
It has a reddish body with a white belly and a white circle around each eye.

✳ BEHAVIOR
It builds nests of leaves and twigs in tree hollows or in upper branches.

✳ MORE
It also eats berries, nuts, mushrooms, insects, and eggs.

GOLDEN-MANTLED GROUND SQUIRREL

 Golden-mantled ground squirrels dig large underground burrows and make nests of dry grasses inside. They sleep in their nests and hide there from predators.

The golden-mantled ground squirrel is longer and plumper than its more common relative, the chipmunk.

FIELD NOTES

In winter the golden-mantled ground squirrel hibernates in a cozy chamber inside its burrow.

WHERE TO FIND:

These squirrels inhabit mountain forests and meadows in western Canada and the U.S.

WHAT TO LOOK FOR:

✳ SIZE
Golden-mantled ground squirrels are about a foot long, including their tails.

✳ COLOR
They are grayish, brown, or tan with striped sides and a hood of reddish gold fur on their heads and shoulders.

✳ BEHAVIOR
They stockpile their favorite foods—seeds, berries, fruits, and insects.

✳ MORE
They are also called golden chipmunks.

RINGTAIL

 At night the ringtail comes out to prowl. It hunts almost anything it can reach, and as an expert climber it can reach a lot! Its back feet can swivel 180 degrees, helping it grip tightly as it climbs.

WHERE TO FIND:
Ringtails live mostly in rocky areas in the southwestern United States and in Mexico.

WHAT TO LOOK FOR:

✳ SIZE
The ringtail is about 30 inches long, including a 15-inch tail.

✳ COLOR
Its body is grayish. The long tail has black and white rings and a black tip.

✳ BEHAVIOR
Ringtails often sleep in trees with their tails hanging down.

✳ MORE
Bobcats and owls are the ringtail's main predators.

Native Americans saw the ringtail's cat-like body and long tail and gave it a name meaning "half a mountain lion."

SNOWSHOE HARE

 Crouched by a snowdrift, the snowshoe hare is nearly invisible. Only its dark eyes and the black tips of its ears give it away. If disturbed, it often runs in big circles, traveling up to 30 miles an hour.

WHERE TO FIND:
You can find snowshoe hares mostly in northern and mountain forests in Canada and the U.S.

WHAT TO LOOK FOR:

✳ SIZE
The snowshoe hare ranges from 15 to 20 inches long, including a 2-inch tail.

✳ COLOR
It is brown in summer and white in winter. In between, its fur changes color gradually.

✳ BEHAVIOR
This shy hare hides most of the day.

✳ MORE
It prefers to eat fresh green plants, but in winter it eats tree buds and bark.

Its summer coat helps this hare hide from predators—bobcats, lynxes, foxes, hawks, wolverines, owls, and weasels.

HOARY MARMOT

A large relative of the squirrel, the hoary (HOR-ee) marmot thrives in the mountains. No cliff or ledge is too high for this chubby rodent. It burrows under rocks for safety from predators.

FIELD NOTES

Hoary marmots often wrestle by pushing against each other with their front feet.

WHERE TO FIND:

Hoary marmots inhabit rocky slopes, cliffs, and high meadows in northwestern Canada and the U.S.

WHAT TO LOOK FOR:

✳ SIZE
Hoary marmots can be 17 to 32 inches long.

✳ COLOR
They have silver-gray bodies with black and white marks on their heads and dark boot-like markings on their feet.

✳ BEHAVIOR
Hoary marmots hibernate in winter.

✳ MORE
They often doze on rocks to feel the warm sun.

The hoary marmot eats a lot of plants, roots, and berries in summer to fatten up for its long winter sleep.

MOUNTAIN GOAT

 High craggy mountains are the realm of the mountain goat. Compact, muscular bodies, short legs, and hoofs made for climbing take mountain goats across cliffs and over peaks. Few enemies can follow.

WHERE TO FIND:
Mountain goats are found in high rocky areas of mountain ranges in western Canada and the U.S.

WHAT TO LOOK FOR:

✳ SIZE
Mountain goats reach three to almost four feet high at the shoulder.

✳ COLOR
They have shaggy white coats. Males and females have sharp black horns.

✳ BEHAVIOR
Mountain goats roam in herds, eating tender grasses and brushy shrubs.

✳ MORE
Golden eagles sometimes carry away mountain goat kids.

Mountain goat young, called kids, can stand, run, and jump shortly after birth.

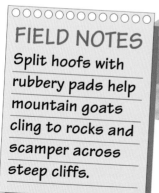

BIGHORN SHEEP

In the fall in the mountains, you may hear a loud crack— the sound of two male bighorn sheep running into each other and butting heads. The males, called rams, fight to show which one is stronger.

Bighorn

Dall's

FIELD NOTES

The horns of a bighorn sheep are thicker and curl more tightly than those of the Dall's sheep.

A ram's horns grow more each year and can weigh up to 30 pounds—as much as all his bones. A female's horns are smaller.

WHAT TO LOOK FOR:

✳ SIZE
Bighorn sheep rams are up to three and a half feet high at the shoulder. Females are shorter.

✳ COLOR
The sheep are brown with white rumps.

✳ BEHAVIOR
Large groups gather in winter, led by an older female, or ewe (YOU).

✳ MORE
Bighorns living in desert areas are paler and thinner.

61

MULE DEER

Mule deer, or muleys, are very social animals. They live in large herds in rugged country. Their big ears are always alert for the sounds of mountain lions or wolves, their chief enemies.

The antlers of this male muley, or buck, are just beginning to grow. They will be full-size by the fall mating season.

WHERE TO FIND:

Mule deer live in mountains, on woody hillsides, and in desert areas of western North America.

WHAT TO LOOK FOR:

✳ SIZE
Mule deer measure about three and a half feet high at the shoulder.

✳ COLOR
They have gray coats that turn red in summer, black tails, and white rumps.

✳ BEHAVIOR
In the fall bucks use their antlers to fight each other to attract females.

✳ MORE
The deer feed mainly at dawn and dusk on trees, shrubs, and grasses.

FIELD NOTES

To escape danger, muleys often bounce away, moving in an unpredictable zigzag pattern.

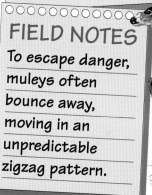

AMERICAN ELK

Elk are very large deer that seem to have a lot to say. In winter and summer they gather in large groups and communicate using many different sounds, including barks, whistles, and cat-like meows.

WHERE TO FIND:
Elk are found on high pastures, wooded slopes, and in forests of western Canada and the U.S.

WHAT TO LOOK FOR:

✷ **SIZE**
A bull elk stands up to five feet at the shoulder. Females are smaller.

✷ **COLOR**
Elk are brown, grayish, or reddish with a paler rump.

✷ **BEHAVIOR**
Males fight each other to win control of females.

✷ **MORE**
Elk are also called wapiti (WAP-ih-tee), an Indian word for "white rump."

Only the male, or bull, elk has antlers. They may be five feet across, with six points, or prongs, on each side.

BOBCAT

 Not much bigger than a house cat, the bobcat is a fierce hunter. Its favorite prey is the cottontail rabbit, but it can also kill a young white-tailed deer. Bobcats sometimes live near cities.

WHERE TO FIND:
Bobcats live in mountain forests, open areas, and many other habitats in much of North America.

WHAT TO LOOK FOR:

✳ SIZE
The bobcat can grow to almost 4 feet long, including a 3- to 7-inch tail.

✳ COLOR
Its fur is grayish to reddish with dark spots.

✳ BEHAVIOR
The female cares for the young. She has two to four kittens in a den on a rock ledge or in a hollow tree or cave.

✳ MORE
Bobcats eat all kinds of mammals.

FIELD NOTES

FIELD NOTES

White on a mother bobcat's ears and tail helps her babies keep her in sight as they follow her.

Adult bobcats live alone. They rely on excellent sight and hearing to find prey, then sneak up and pounce to capture it.

67

GRAY WOLF

A gray wolf knows its place. Most gray wolves live in packs that travel and hunt together. Each wolf shows respect for the strongest male—the leader of the pack—and for his mate.

WHERE TO FIND:
Gray wolves live in open forests and on tundra, mostly in Canada and Alaska.

WHAT TO LOOK FOR:

＊SIZE
A gray wolf measures up to six and a half feet long.

＊COLOR
Its fur ranges from white to black.

＊BEHAVIOR
By hunting in packs, wolves can kill a moose or other animal ten times the size of a single wolf.

＊MORE
People sometimes hunt wolves because they kill cows and other livestock.

The wolf is the largest kind of wild dog. Some gray wolves have black or reddish fur.

MOUNTAIN LION

 The mountain lion is a loner. It roams mountain forests by itself, hunting deer and other mammals by day and by night. It gets together with other mountain lions only at mating time.

WHERE TO FIND:
These cats live in western mountain areas, forests, and swamps from Canada through Central America.

WHAT TO LOOK FOR:

✳ SIZE
A mountain lion can be six feet long and have a tail more than two feet long.

✳ COLOR
They are tan or gray with paler chests and bellies.

✳ BEHAVIOR
Mountain lions do not roar. They sound like house cats, only louder.

✳ MORE
They are also called pumas, cougars, and panthers.

One mountain lion kills about 30 deer a year. It eats all it wants, hides the remains, and returns to the kill to feed when it is hungry.

BLACK BEAR

During the summer black bears spend a lot of time eating. They consume up to 18 pounds of food each day to fatten up for the winter. Then, most bears settle down in their dens and rest.

FIELD NOTES

This bear loves honey. Its thick hair helps protect it from stinging bees when it raids a hive.

Bears have poor eyesight, but their large sensitive noses help them find the food they need.

WHERE TO FIND:
Black bears can be found in forests and swamps across Canada and in parts of the United States and Mexico.

WHAT TO LOOK FOR:

✳ SIZE
Black bears can be up to 6 feet long and weigh almost 600 pounds.

✳ COLOR
Often black, the bears can also be brown or even dingy white.

✳ BEHAVIOR
Black bears become inactive during the winter.

✳ MORE
They eat plants, berries, insects, other mammals, fish, birds, and carrion.

GRIZZLY BEAR

Grizzlies are immense brown bears. Everything about them is big, from their tall, bulky bodies to their huge, wide heads and powerful claws that measure up to four inches long.

You can tell a grizzly from a black bear by the grizzly's humped shoulders.

WHERE TO FIND:
Grizzlies inhabit mountains, coasts, and river areas of northwestern North America.

WHAT TO LOOK FOR:

✳ SIZE
The grizzly can measure up to 10 feet long and weigh up to 1,700 pounds.

✳ COLOR
Its long coat is usually brown and often grizzled, or tipped with gray.

✳ BEHAVIOR
Grizzlies head for a river to fish when salmon are migrating upstream.

✳ MORE
They rest in dens in winter but waken easily when disturbed.

FIELD NOTES

A grizzly often bites and claws tree trunks to let other bears know it claims an area as its territory.

GLOSSARY

adapt To change over a long period of time in response to a certain environment or set of conditions.

amphibian A cold-blooded animal, such as a toad or salamander, that has moist skin without scales and lays its eggs in water.

antlers A pair of bony growths on the heads of most kinds of male deer that are shed each year.

carrion Dead and rotting animals.

conifer A tree or shrub, such as a pine, that grows cones and has needle-like leaves.

hibernate To enter an inactive, sleep-like state with lowered body temperature.

mammal A warm-blooded animal, usually with hair or fur, that feeds its young on milk from the mother's body.

migrate To move from one area to another, usually in the spring and fall.

plumage A bird's feathers.

predator An animal that hunts and kills other animals for food.

prey An animal that is hunted by other animals for food.

reptile A cold-blooded animal that has scaly or leathery skin and usually lays eggs. Lizards and snakes are reptiles.

territory An area claimed and defended by an animal or a group of animals.

tundra A cold treeless land on the upper slopes of high mountains and in Arctic regions.

INDEX OF
MOUNTAIN LIFE

ABOUT THE CONSULTANTS

Ronald M. Nowak worked as a zoologist in the endangered species program of the U.S. Fish and Wildlife Service for 24 years. The author of the fourth and fifth editions of *Walker's Mammals of the World,* he is currently preparing the sixth edition. He has published some 70 papers, articles, and books of scientific and popular interest.

George E. Watson served as Curator of Birds in the Smithsonian Institution's National Museum of Natural History from 1962 to 1985. A fellow and past secretary and vice president of the American Ornithologists' Union, he has been a member of the National Geographic Society's Committee for Research and Exploration since 1975.

PHOTOGRAPHIC CREDITS